Today meets Yesterday

For Onno & Immi

In 1868, the Chinese emperor sent an envoy by the name of Zhi Gang (志刚) to America and then to Europe to report back on industrialization. Impressed, the scholar told of technological progress and modern production processes, but also of the loss of human values, the pure pursuit of material wealth, and the disappearance of reason. Zhi Gang, like other envoys, feared an excessive use of resources and machines, which replace people more and more and push them out of the focus of creative work. Rather than concentrating on real needs everything was about profit. This way of life went against the traditional Chinese concept of existing in lasting harmony with nature and the heavens.

On the topic of change, opinions have always differed widely. While some delight in progress and the innovations it brings, other mourn after tradition and the good old days. Technological developments obviously bring us many positive advantages, particularly where everyday comforts are concerned. They have come to define lifestyles in big cities all over the world and are now considered status symbols.

Nowadays, we hardly have to move anymore and manage our entire lives with one tiny device. We have come—at least technologically speaking—farther within the past 200 years, than in the millennia before. We have friends around the globe; people from all over the world "like" our posts and can take part in our daily lives. We love transparency and value a hierarchy-free society. An immeasurable amount of information streams through the internet—it seems endless. Our computers are

onstantly getting faster; human efficiency seems capable of increas-
ng ad infinitum.

What happens in and with us in times like these? How do we handle our
hanging environment? What exactly are the differences between back
hen and today? What are the changes doing to our society? How are our
abits, perceptions, political stances, our values, and lastly, our view of
he world changing? Could it be that, along with the many benefits we
ope to gain from progress and those that have already manifested, some
f the fears held by the Chinese envoy 150 years ago have come true?

hree years ago, I began documenting these changes through my per-
onal experiences and perceptions in pictures. They have been gathered
n this book and will hopefully inspire further conversation and exchange.

Breakfast

Circle of friends

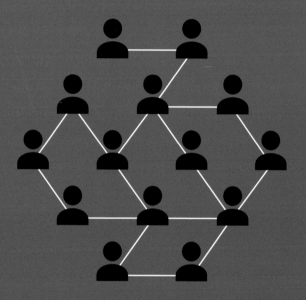

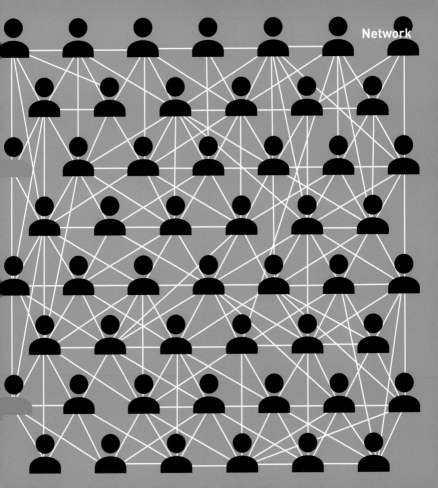

Network

Shopping

Coffee

Noise

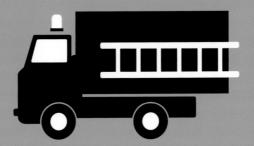

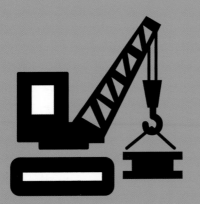

f

 in

Concert

Concert

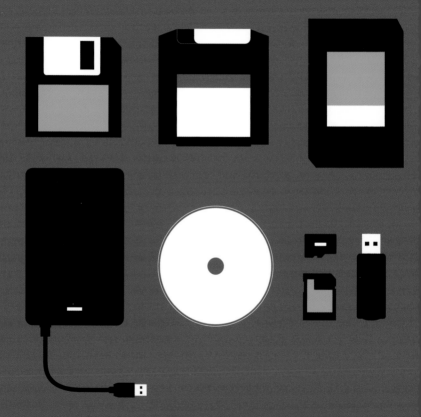

Storage media

Cell phones

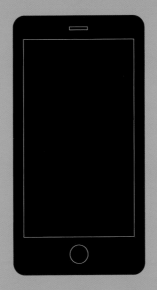

Meeting with friends

Metropolises

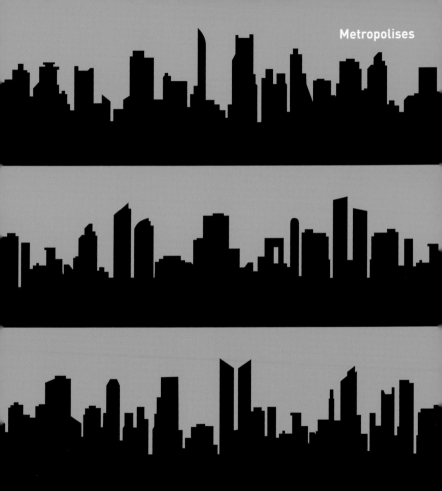

Metropolises

1945

need

buy

toss

today

need

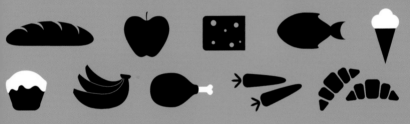

buy

toss

Packaging waste

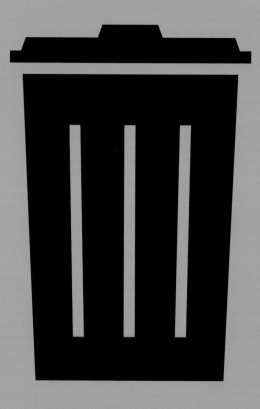

City – suburbs – country

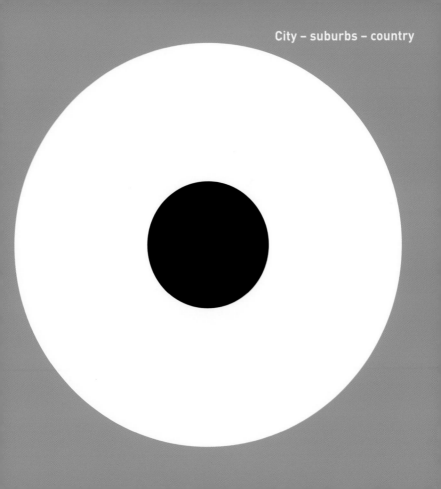

Running

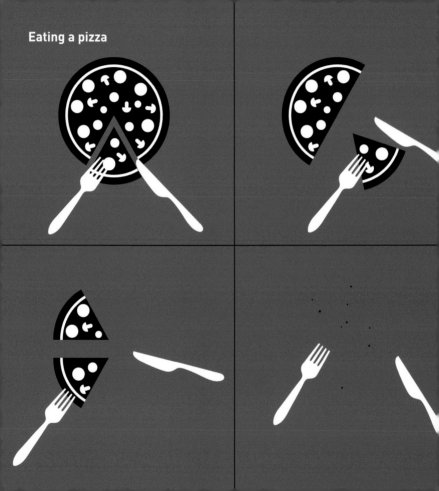

Eating a pizza

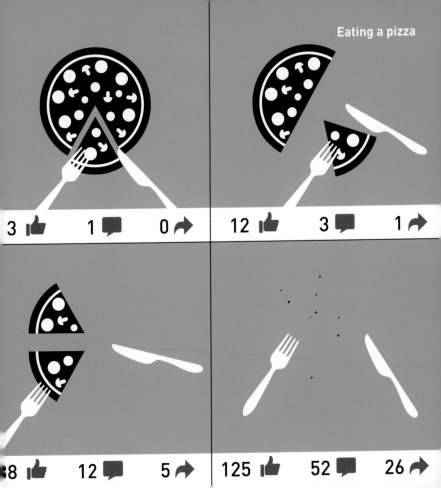

Eating a pizza

3 👍 1 💬 0 ➡

12 👍 3 💬 1 ➡

8 👍 12 💬 5 ➡

125 👍 52 💬 26 ➡

1965

healthy

unhealthy

healthy

unhealthy

Demonstration

Playing

Shortsightedness among children

Cucumbers

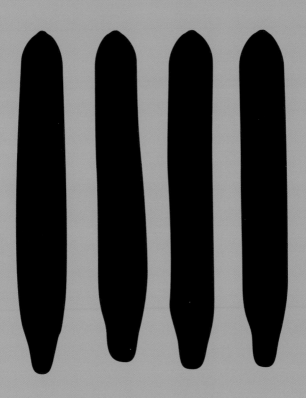

Product testing

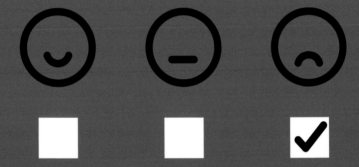

Artisanry

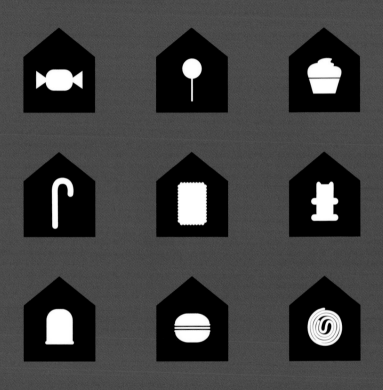

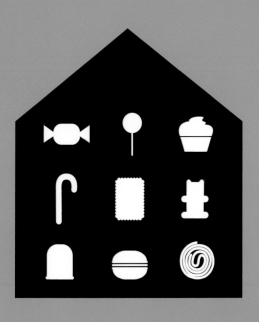

Concentration

Individual

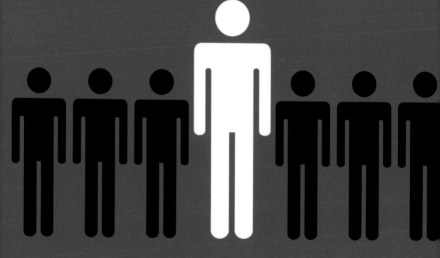

Boss

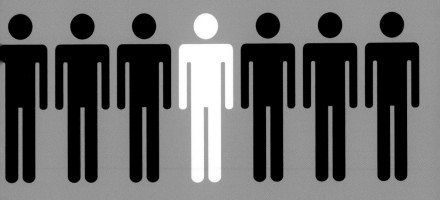

Formation of worldview

Leisure – work

Work – leisure

Knowledge

My idea

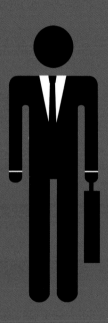

Bank loan

Countryside – city

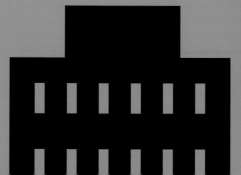

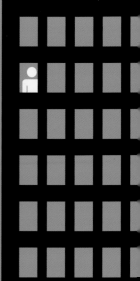

City – countryside

Photo

Bullying

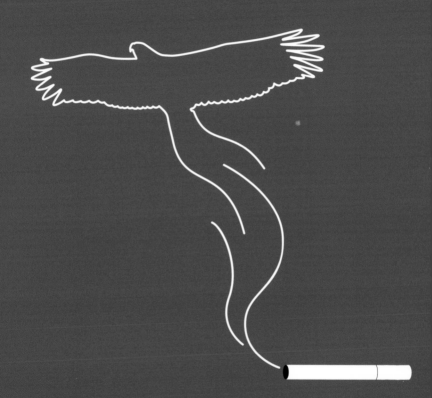

Feeling alive

Fur

Fur

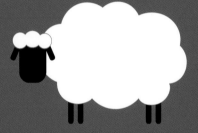

Dolly

Military intervention

Tax evasion

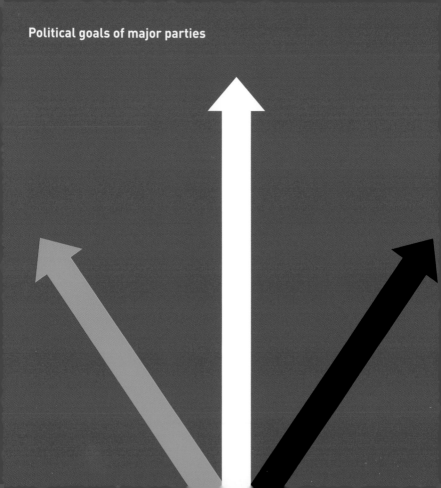

Political goals of major parties

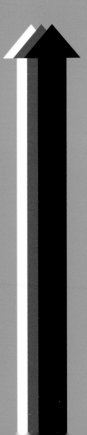

Political goals of major parties

Center ground

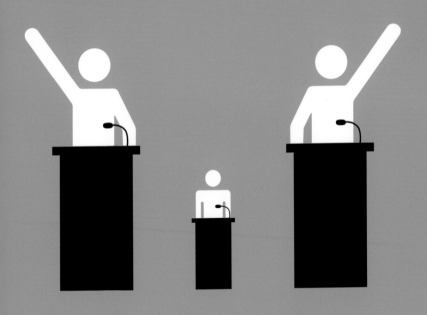

Difference rich – poor

Oceans

Oceans

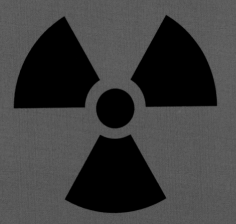

Chernobyl 1986

Fukushima 2011

The Arctic

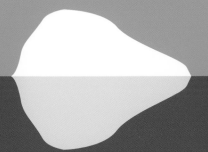

Industrialized countries – rest of the world

Western perception of the Middle East

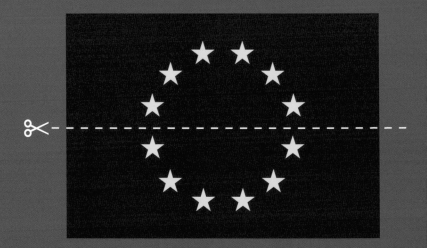

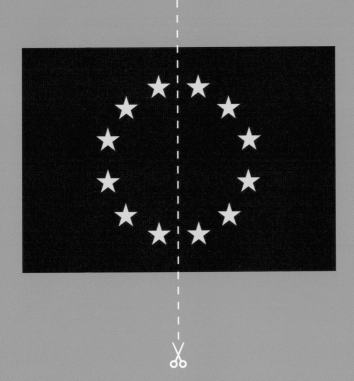

Capitalism – Socialism

Power

$

Children – adults

1700

1900

Children – adults

1960

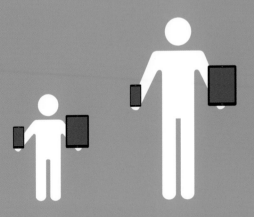

today

Energy

Energy

Gender equality

Gender equality

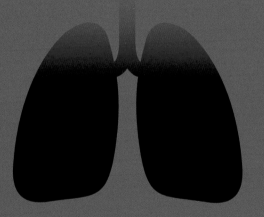

Industrial age – black lung

Digital age – burnout

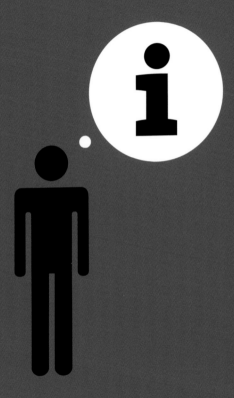

Threats

Past – present – future

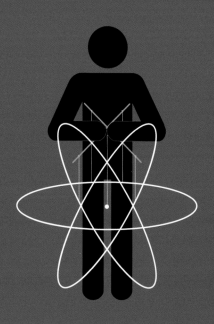

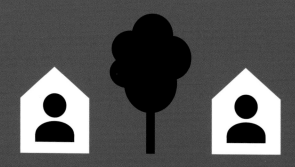

Neighbors

Opposition

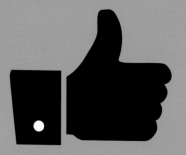

Exploitation

Self-fulfillment

Danger

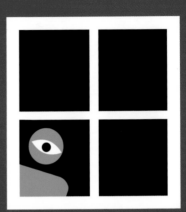

Privacy

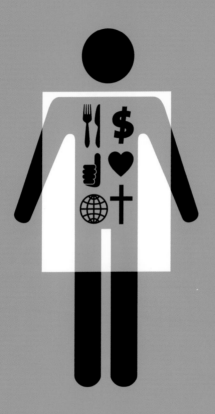

Roots

Multicultural

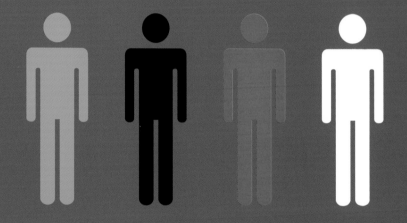

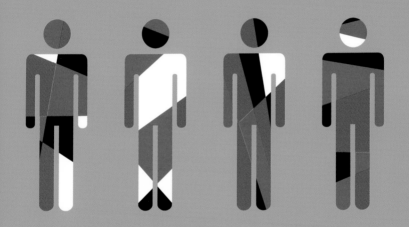

Other books by Yang Liu:

East meets West · 东西相遇
Yang Liu · 刘扬

TASCHEN

"For a generation that increasingly uses emoticons that say much more than words, these books could be the future."
—*Show Daily*, New Delhi

Man meets Woman
Yang Liu

TASCHEN

"...sure to have you laughing at, celebrating and pondering the differences between men and women."
—*Psychologies*, Kent

ang Liu was born in 1976 in Beijing. After studying at the University of rts Berlin (UdK), she worked as a designer in Singapore, London, Berin, and New York. In 2004 she founded her own design studio, which she ontinues to run today. In addition to holding workshops and lectures at nternational conferences, she has taught at numerous universities in ermany and abroad. In 2010 she was appointed a professor at the BTK niversity of Applied Sciences in Berlin. Her works have won numerous rizes in international competitions and can be found in museums and ollections all over the world.

ang Liu lives and works in Berlin.

Today meets yesterday
A book by **Yang Liu**

Idea/Design © Yang Liu

© Copyright of all
artwork and text by
Yang Liu Design
Torstraße 185 · 10115 Berlin
www.yangliudesign.com

Project Management:
Florian Kobler, Berlin
Production: Daniela Asmuth, Cologne
English translation: Hayley Haupt, Ixelles

© 2016 TASCHEN GmbH
Hohenzollernring 53 · 50672 Cologne
www.taschen.com

ISBN 978-3-8365-5405-3

Printed in Italy